THE ART OF
CENTRAL AFRICA

THE ART OF
CENTRAL AFRICA

Sculpture and Tribal Masks

INTRODUCTION BY
WILLIAM FAGG

A MENTOR-UNESCO ART BOOK

PUBLISHED BY
THE NEW AMERICAN LIBRARY, NEW YORK AND TORONTO
BY ARRANGEMENT WITH UNESCO

FIRST PRINTING, DECEMBER, 1967

MENTOR TRADEMARK REG. U. S. PAT. OFF. AND FOREIGN COUNTRIES
REGISTERED TRADEMARK—MARCA REGISTRADA

MENTOR-UNESCO ART BOOKS ARE PUBLISHED IN THE UNITED STATES BY
THE NEW AMERICAN LIBRARY, INC.,
1301 AVENUE OF THE AMERICAS, NEW YORK, NEW YORK 10019,
IN CANADA BY THE NEW AMERICAN LIBRARY OF CANADA LIMITED,
295 KING STREET EAST, TORONTO 2, ONTARIO
PRINTED IN ITALY BY AMILCARE PIZZI S.P.A. MILANO

I n *The Art of Western Africa* we surveyed briefly, from west to east, some of the principal art styles of the great West African area which stretches from Senegal to the Grasslands of Cameroon, stopping short of the Sanaga River. The Sanaga, flowing into the Gulf of Guinea near Duala, provides a convenient boundary between the two great halves of the sculpture-producing area of Africa associated respectively with the Niger and Congo river systems. And in terms of art, the division is a real and not merely an arbitrary one, since the Sanaga Valley forms a " no man's land " from which (except near its mouth) little or no art has been reported. We can now proceed to examine some of the Congo styles.

The small Duala tribe, living in and around the town of that name, are perhaps in an ambiguous position between the Niger and Congo spheres of art, as their carvings do not present an obvious relationship to the nearest neighbouring styles on either side. But their traditional origins suggest that they may be conveniently allotted to the Congo group.

Duala art takes two main forms. Their finest works, very few in number, are certain beautifully elaborated canoe-prow ornaments—for the Duala are great boatmen and their regattas are famous. They were made in the nineteenth century in a remarkably fluent openwork style which reminds one of *art nouveau*, of old Maori openwork carving and of the art of the Bush Negroes of Surinam (which may indeed owe more to the Duala than to any of the other West African tribes which contributed to that hybrid population). In our century, this excellence of design has largely disappeared, probably under the seductive influence of European oil paints.

The other important art form of the Duala—and one which has similarly suffered in recent times from acculturation by paint—is the mask type which we illustrate in Plate 1. It is of the horizontal type, like some found at several other points on the West African coast, and in most or all cases appears to represent an antelope. The decoration is boldly geometrical, and predominantly in white, red and black.

We come next to a tribal complex whose best sculptors were by common consent among Africa's greatest: the Fang. They inhabit the southern part of Cameroon, Spanish Guinea (Rio Muni) and northern Gabon, but are said to be comparative newcomers to the area, having arrived less than two hundred years ago after a drive from the far interior to the sea, which they reached only about 1870-90. (The name " Fang " is here used for the whole group, including the Bulu and Beti. It is, however, strictly applied by themselves only to the main southern section, no indigenous generic term being available; the old-fashioned terms " Pahouin " and " Pangwe " are less correct versions of the same word.) The art of the Fang presents us with some extremely puzzling enigmas and paradoxes of a historical kind, which are given their importance precisely because of the exceptionally high qualities of the sculptures.

The movements of the Fang groups during the nineteenth century are fairly well established, from their crossing of the upper Sanaga about 1800 through their southward drive until they reached the Atlantic Ocean on the Gabon coast towards the end of the century. But it is thought that they may have come originally from the region of the Nile-Congo watershed, near the home of the Mangbetu and Azande. Evidence from the comparison of artistic forms tends to confirm this view, for several tribes in the northern parts of the Congo stylize the human face in a similar way to the Fang sculptors. Such spectacular progress across the continent is in keeping with the energetic character of this warrior tribe.

6

If, without already knowing something of their art, one were to attempt to forecast the kind of art which such a tribe would produce, it would surely be reasonable to say, first, that if they had been on the move for perhaps two or three centuries through a hostile environment it would be most unusual for them to have produced any sculpture at all, beyond small and portable personal charms; and, secondly, that, if they had done so, one might expect their way of life to be reflected in a fierce and horrific expressionism such as is found in some masks of the Ngere of the Ivory Coast or the Basonge of the eastern Congo. Yet in fact Fang sculpture appears to most observers to be the most deeply serene of African styles, based on a quietistic humanism, and positively therapeutic in its freedom from aggression. Moreover, it is extremely difficult to think of it as an art of recent origin or development rather than the culmination of an ancient tradition; the great dealer Paul Guillaume was led by their appearance of antiquity to commit himself to some highly fanciful datings (to the thirteenth, tenth and even sixth centuries) for some of the best Fang works.

For these and other reasons we have here a mystery as great as that of the Ife naturalism which we met in *The Art of Western Africa*. Can it be that, while the Fang oral traditions reflect as usual the history of the ruling newcomers, the art is that of an indigenous people into whose culture the invaders quickly became assimilated?

The most important Fang sculptures are funerary heads (Plate 2) and figures (said by some informants to be later than the heads) which were affixed to the cylindrical bark reliquaries for the skulls and small bones of ancestors in order to ward off evil influences. In spite of their very real presence, it is said that these carvings are not representations of the deceased, that is, of the immediate ancestors of the family; but they are nevertheless to be regarded as ancestor figures, for they represent the original ancestors of the family or the clan. Plate 3 illustrates another impressive type of figure, carved from softer wood and painted white (rather than stained to a dark colour by constant applications of palm oil), and apparently not designed to be fixed to the reliquaries.

The problems of Fang art become further complicated when we compare it with that of the Bakota, their neighbours to the south-east. As with the Fang, the principal art form of the Bakota is a guardian figure placed in the receptacle of the ancestors' bones on the family shrine; but, whereas the *bieri* of the Fang is a fully rounded sculpture, strongly suggestive of human flesh, skin and bone, the *mbulu-ngulu* of the Bakota is a thoroughly schematized abstraction, hardly departing from a two-dimensional plane. (Both these art forms, we may note, exerted a profound influence on modern European artists, the Fang chiefly on sculptors such as Epstein, the Bakota rather on painters such as Picasso). The identical function of the two kinds of figure supports the suggestion that the Fang style may have been adopted from the existing population rather than introduced by the Fang invaders.

Plate 4 is a classical example of the Bakota style, with its brass and copper sheeting. There are many other substyles which provide variations on the same theme; the most striking among them is the substyle usually attributed to the Osyeba, a marginal group between Fang and Bakota whose general cultural affinities are uncertain, though in art at least they seem closer to the Bakota. Plate 5 illustrates this highly original conception of the human head, which to a western eye suggests some monstrous sting-ray; the effect is enhanced by the plating, made up of narrow strips of copper.

The neighbours of the Fang to the east (and of the Bakota to the north) are the Bakwele, whose culture is said to have been strongly influenced by the Fang in the nineteenth century, but whose art shows little sign of this—no doubt because activities which are backed by effective religious sanctions are more resistant to change. Bakwele art is virtually confined to masks of human and animal forms in a highly characteristic style which has produced some of Africa's finest sculptures. The head is drastically simplified, with a concave face in which the placing of the features, especially the long pod-like eyes, calls for great artistic sensitivity on the part of the carver. The woodcarving illustrated in Plate 6 is not a mask in the strict sense, as it is janiform, that is, it has identical faces on each side of a block of wood 10 cm thick, and no apertures for vision. Nor does it bear any evidence of the manner in which it was used; it may, therefore, perhaps be comparable to certain Baule " masks " which were made not for use but for display only. But it is nevertheless a good specimen of Bakwele design. The style is seen at its finest in the antelope mask in Plate 7, which was doubtless meant to be worn on the forehead of the dancer at an angle to the ground of about 45°. Like all Bakwele masks it is strongly symmetrical and there is a dominant emphasis on the exponential form of the horns; in fact, these beautiful curves of growth impart a supple fluency to the composition which seems to override the basically two-dimensional form of the mask as a whole.

As every fieldworker well knows from his own experience, it is a fact that an arrangement in order of artistic merit of sculptures from a given tribal community will be much the same whether the evaluation is made by an informed and unprejudiced western observer such as himself or by artists, patrons or other members of the community concerned (always provided that extraneous ethnographical phenomena, such as some iconographical error or omission, have not inhibited or distorted the appreciation by these latter of the universal values whose existence is implied in this statement—for the art historian's analytical distinction between subject-matter and style is of course not used in tribal society). A statistically controlled experiment to test this proposition was recently carried out among the Bakwele by the American scholar Siroto, who collected photographs of as many Bakwele masks as possible and submitted them to critical evaluation first in the Department of Fine Arts at Yale University and secondly by various groups of Bakwele. The degree of concordance was remarkable, and the few discrepancies were for the most part readily explicable by extraneous factors. Proof of this kind was needed for the enlightenment of sceptics and philistines.

The next stylistic area, immediately to the south of the Fang and to the west of the Bakota tribes, is made up of many small tribes speaking related languages and sharing, as their main art form, the well-known white-faced masks of which one is shown in Plate 8. Innumerable examples of such masks are known, but very few are properly documented (and indeed by no means all are genuine). The tribes concerned (including the Mpongwe, the Galoa, the Ashira, the Mashango, the Bapunu, the Balumbo, the Banjabi and the Batsangi) thus present a problem of identification comparable to that found in the Grasslands of Cameroon, though we do not know whether it is similarly complicated by intertribal trading in works of art. It would seem that the region contains large areas of uninhabited forest, which have no doubt inhibited comprehensive study of the arts of the area, and may also account for the fact that, from the nineteenth century onwards, a great many of the masks seem to have been brought to the coast for sale, rather than collected in the interior. For this reason, they have usually been published as Mpongwe or, more recently, Balumbo; these tribes, at the northern and southern ends of the coast respectively, are commonly made to stand for the whole group of " Ogowe River tribes ".

The example illustrated in Plate 8, which is attributed to the Bapunu, is fairly typical of the numerous variations on the theme which occur in the area, and the prominent scarifications—nine keloids or artificial scars arranged in lozenge formation in the centre of the forehead, and others in rectangular formation in the region between ear and eye —are found, probably, on the majority of the " white-faced masks ". The Mongoloid appearance of the rather naturalistic and fleshy face is equally characteristic (and it should be said at once that there is no reason whatever for us to attempt to explain it by Asiatic contact or influence). And the centrally lobed coiffure is a surprisingly constant feature, found equally in documented masks of this type which have been collected in the Bakota country. We cannot tell, with our present knowledge, whether this art form spread rapidly, perhaps as late as the nineteenth century, from one of these small tribes to the rest, together, presumably, with the dance society (called Mukui in some at least of the tribes) for which it was made; or whether it is of more ancient origin and is undergoing a process of differentiation. But on the artistic evidence it seems at least possible that the Ogowe tribes, like the Fang complex, should be considered as one great but nameless unit divided into a number of named sections.

In our next artistic province we are confronted once again with a group of peoples related by culture and language and practising a single style of art with local variations; but in this case it is quite clear that they form a single great tribe or tribal complex—the Bakongo—uniting in a single cultural entity all the groups comprised in the old kingdom of Kongo and its associated states, including (besides the group called simply the Bakongo) the Bavili, the Mayombe, the Kakongo, the Bawoyo, the Basolongo, the Basundi, the Badondo or Babwende and the Baladi. We do not know when the Kongo kingdom was established, but it was probably a century or two before the Portuguese arrived in the late fifteenth century. It was, and for some time remained, a highly centralized state, and this applied also to most of the western Congo states. A king of the requisite calibre could exercise almost absolute power, the monarchy being in this respect closer to the Benin type than to the more constitutional Yoruba type. But from the later sixteenth century onwards, Kongo was more and more weakened by attack and attrition both from Portuguese intrigues and from the Jaga invasions from the far interior; the power of the king waned and was extinguished, distributing itself among a large number of petty kingships, each holding sway over a few villages only, somewhat on the Yoruba pattern.

It seems highly improbable that this long drawn-out process of political disintegration could have been accompanied, in the field of art (usually so responsive to socio-political change), by increasing stylistic integration and assimilation throughout the former imperial domains. Consequently, we must assume that the artistic homogeneity of the Bakongo peoples was established in the fifteenth century or earlier, when the great kings were consolidating their rule over the kingdom of Kongo and their leadership over the associated states such as Loango. By the sixteenth century, when the kings had embraced Christianity, their influence was directed towards the suppression of the pagan religion and art rather than to their development, though the tendencies to conformity in the general culture of the component tribes and subtribes could not have failed to affect the tribal art in some degree. From this argument it would follow that the naturalism which is the most obvious characteristic of the art of the Bakongo tribes today was already well established before the arrival of the first Portuguese under Diogo Cão in 1482; the artistic ideas imported soon thereafter by the missionaries would have been those of the High Renaissance, and the chance affinity between these and the tribal art must certainly have allowed of influences flowing from the former to the latter, leading to a further refinement of naturalism.

If this conjectural interpretation of the art history of the Bakongo is correct (and it could be established only by the excavation of Bakongo sculptures, probably of stone, in deposits positively datable to the pre-European period), then the survival into the twentieth century of the stylistic unity of the Bakongo group is surely very remarkable. It may be taken as a sign both of the great and widespread prestige and of the inherent artistic strength of the style —perhaps most notably demonstrated in the clear derivation from the sixteenth-century kingdom of Kongo of the royal sculptures of the Bakuba of Kasai (see Plate 18) and, still more clearly, of the Bakuba decorative style as seen in their famous raffia pile embroideries and carved cups, boxes and other utensils.

The qualities of the Bakongo artists at their best are finely exemplified in Plate 9, and above all their capacity for the harmonious reconciliation of naturalism with stylization. This is seen particularly clearly in the design of the neck, which is not as in nature, but is an inverted and truncated cone, of a kind now much used in the support of great modern buildings in the manner of Le

Two soapstone ancestor figures. Height: 41 and 40 cm. Perhaps seventeenth or eighteenth century A.D. Bakongo tribe, northern Angola. (British Museum, London. Photo: William Fagg.)

Corbusier. Indeed, this illustration might serve to epitomize the qualities in African art which so fired the imagination of the pioneer modern artists in France and Germany around the turn of the century. The pieces of iron driven into the trunk show that this work is a true "fetish" (an impersonal instrument for the control, for good or bad purposes, of the life force) rather than an ancestor figure. A noble old fragment of such a *konde* fetish appears in Plate 10; this piece was illustrated in the first book on negro art to be published under the influence of the modern art movement, Carl Einstein's *Negerplastik* (1915). Such *konde* fetishes are used mainly for offensive purposes; *moganga* fetishes, such as the very complete example seen in Plate 11, are beneficent and are variously used for curative and protective purposes. The extremely rare figure shown in Plate 12, although it has been attributed to the Babembe, may rather originate from the Badondo (or Babwende); with three or four other unidentified but clearly related pieces, having similar scarification and the same peculiar conformation of the shoulders and arms, it appears to be related to one of the most extraordinary, yet little known, manifestations of art in all Africa—the enormous funerary figures of stuffed red cloth formerly carried in funerals, as receptacles for the remains of the deceased, by the Badondo and sometimes by the Basundi. These figures, which may exceed 10 metres in height and are broad in proportion, exhibit the same angular treatment of the arms.

Among a number of important tribes living to the east of the Bakongo (including the Bayaka, Basuku and Bambala, all showing the effects of influence from the kingdom of Kongo) we now select the Bapende, who occupy a large area—or rather three loosely connected areas, a western, a northern and a south-eastern—to the west of the Bakuba. From their traditions it appears that they began as a southern component of the Kongo kingdom, whence they migrated in the sixteenth and seventeenth centuries by way of the Kwango to the tract between the Kwilu and Kasai rivers, being regarded by their neighbours on the way as bringers of higher culture. But once in their new

14

home they came under Lunda rule and abandoned the traditions of their own distinguished past in favour of the clan traditions of their new rulers.

Fortunately, the art of the Bapende has been admirably studied in the field by Father de Sousberghe. It is known above all for its rich development of the dance mask (*mbuya*) for use chiefly in connection with initiation. The classical form of mask is that found especially in the northern section of the tribe west of the Loange, and made in and around the Katundu chiefdom; the example shown in Plate 13 appears to represent either *fumu*, the chief, or *phumbu*, the executioner. The Katundu type of mask, with its prominent forehead and strongly marked brow ridge, was sometimes made also for the south-eastern group on the left bank of the Kasai, whose own most characteristic form, however, was a flat, triangular mask with more stylized features. The helmet mask called *giphogo* (Plate 14) is found only in this south-eastern section of the tribe. Like almost all Bapende sculptures—and indeed like their own bodies—it is predominantly coloured a bright red, obtained from red ochre or from powdered cam wood.

Tukula or *ngula*, the powdered red cam wood, will serve as a transitional motif as we pass on to the art of the Bakuba and the " Bakuba-ized " tribes of Kasai Province, for although they do not cover their whole bodies with it as the Bapende so often do, it is their most prized possession, and in the less developed parts of the Bakuba country it is still a principal medium of trade. Little study has been given to the colour preferences of African tribes, but there is no doubt that among the Bakuba (as among the Russians) the colour red has an intimate connection with the concept of beauty. *Tukula* is indeed used as a modelling material in their most abstract form of sculpture, the beautifully decorated gifts presented to mourners at important funerals.

The Bakuba are a great tribal complex occupying a central position near the northern limits of the central African savannah, chiefly in the area between the middle Kasai and the lower Sankuru. The complex consists of about a dozen subtribes or sections, some of them of alien origin, such as the Bakete or the Babinji; but they have been welded into a single cultural entity with rather slight local differences, under the dominating influence of the royal subtribe, known variously as Bambala, Bushongo or Baphila. Their oral history purports to go back, through 124 named kings, to about A.D. 500, but it is improbable that any great credence should be placed in the list before the seventeenth century. Even for the last three centuries or so, the traditions should undoubtedly be understood as referring primarily to the royal lineages rather than to the Bakuba as a whole; and before that time there are likely to have been occasions when immigrant kings inflated the king list by interpolating their own ancestors—so that parts of it, to use an electrical metaphor, ought perhaps to be read " in parallel " rather than " in series ". The old view, propounded by Torday, that the Bakuba migrated with their culture from the far north near Lake Chad quite early in the Christian era no longer appears tenable (though it is just possible that some element of the tribe originated in that region before being assimilated into the culture of the remainder). More recent research, both on traditional evidence and on the internal evidence of the material culture, has established that Bakuba culture is very largely of western origin and in particular that its more advanced features were strongly influenced by the kingdom of Kongo, probably in the sixteenth and seventeenth centuries, in the period associated with the name of their great king and " culture hero " Shamba Bolongongo—who may, it now seems, have come to the Bakuba from one of their westward neighbours, the Bambunda or the Badinga.

Of all African art styles, none has placed so great an emphasis upon the decorative as that of the Bakuba. Its pre-eminence in this field is comparable to that of Maori art in the Pacific. The Bakuba, like the Maori, are by no means devoid of a feeling for sculptural form, as is shown not only by their royal statues and their masks but also by the forms of their utensils and weapons, both functional and ceremonial; but these are made the vehicle of elaborate decorative designs of characteristic virtuosity which tend to overshadow the formal qualities of the works.

It is noticeable that the same corpus of named and well-defined decorative designs is drawn upon by the Bakuba craftsmen in whatever medium they practise—whether in wood and ivory carving, cam wood and palm-oil paste, raffia textiles and matting, or body scarification. From even a brief study of these media it becomes clear that the designs must have been conceived in terms of textile techniques and then transplanted to the other materials. Here is good confirmation of the derivation of the Bakuba decorative style from the kingdom of Kongo, for raffia pile cloths made by the same technique and having similar or even identical designs were brought from the coastal kingdom in the seventeenth century, if not before, and are preserved at Copenhagen, London, Ulm and Rome. Moreover, in the Kongo kingdom also, textile patterns were reproduced in other materials, notably in ivory; and the same is true of some intervening tribes such as the Bambunda.

Whereas most Bakuba decorative work on wood is carved in low relief, on masks it is commonly carried out in painted colour only, as in Plates 15 and 16, representing two versions of their best-known type of mask. Plate 15 shows the classical version found especially among the Bambala or royal subtribe, and called Ngadi Mwashi after the wife (and incestuous sister) of the primordial ancestor Woto; the version with perforations encircling the eyes (Plate 16) is that used by the Babende society among the eastern subtribe, who call it Shene Malula. The decorative motif of massed triangles found on both is probably derived from coloured and sewn patchwork barkcloth rather than from designs embroidered on woven cloth. The sculptural features—the splayed forehead and the joined nose and mouth—are characteristic of the rather stereo-typed Bakuba convention. The cylindrical helmet mask in Plate 17, with its more grotesque appearance and beard, is said to come from the Bakete, one of the assimilated subtribes which appear to be of alien origin.

The wooden figure (Plate 18) of King Misha Pelenge Che

(c. 1810) is one of nine authentic royal portrait statues surviving from the period before the inauguration of the tourist industry about 1913, since which time innumerable imitations of varying craftsmanship have been produced. Not only the subject-matter of these figures but their rather naturalistic style seem to derive from the chiefs' portraits in stone and wood of the Bakongo, who are said to have used them as surrogates for the chief during his absences on tour or after his death. Among the Bakuba, the figures played a vital part in the transfer of the divine wisdom and powers from a dead king to his successor.

Historically important though they are, the Bakuba royal figures are perhaps rather lacking in sculptural strength. This quality is pre-eminent, however, in the corresponding chiefly figures of the Ndengese, one of the " Bakuba-ized " tribes living on the Lukenye to the north of the Sankuru. Whether these figures were inspired by the court art of the Bakuba or not, their strongly conceptualized torsos and firm design (see Plate 19) give them a more powerful impression of contained force, which puts them on a level with the best Fang figures.

Along the southern fringes of the Bakuba in the valley of the Lulua live the Bena Lulua together with the closely related Bakwa Luntu and Bashilange. The Bena Lulua are cited by Vansina as a case of a tribe which did not come into existence until 1885-90, when the people formerly known as Luba Kasai moved, under pressure from the Basongye, and concentrated around Luluabourg, adopting the name of the river. This may well be true in a political sense, but as an artistic entity their case would seem to be almost the opposite: this same period marks the virtual end of their art history, after which no more figures were carved. It is true that up to this point von Wissmann and other explorers write of them as simply a section of the great Baluba tribal complex, but their art is *sui generis* and among the most distinctive and beautiful of all African styles, and has only a tenuous relationship with the Baluba styles, of which it cannot reasonably be regarded as a mere variant. It seems likely that while they had formed part of the great Baluba military confederacy which began

18

in the sixteenth century, they were never assimilated in a cultural sense but retained their peculiar art style and iconography. Of our two illustrations, the smaller (Plate 20) shows affinity with pieces identified as from the Bakwa Luntu but, like that seen in Plate 21, well exemplifies the characteristic Bena Lulua fusion or reconciliation of sculptural form with surface enhancement. Olbrechts was probably right to class them rather with the Bakuba (with whom they share certain mask types) than with the Baluba; and indeed many of the beautifully decorated drinking horns collected among the Bakuba seem to have been carved by Bena Lulua artists.

The Baluba of south-eastern Congo present another interesting art-historical problem, comparable in some ways with that of the Fang peoples in the north-west. On the one hand, the common elements of style which, as with the Yoruba of Nigeria, enable us to regard the art of the Baluba as a single complex appear to have arisen from the homogenizing effects upon the component peoples of long association in a military empire. On the other hand, the surviving sculpture which was produced in this situation—presumably all to be dated after the mid-nineteenth century—exhibits, in all its varied substyles, just the qualities of gentle and tranquil beauty, of therapeutic reconciliation of forms rather than their violent opposition, which one would not expect in such a context. It is probably unprofitable to speculate further on the causes of the paradox, for we have no means of knowing whether this special informing character of Baluba art was established before the rise of centralized military power.

It may be said that the central sculptural concept of the Baluba is the sphere—not in the sense that spheres actually form part of their sculptures, but rather that the idea of the sphere exerts a kind of attraction, as of gravity, on all their forms—just as the art forms of the neighbouring Basongye tend to be influenced by the idea of the cube (except in those frontier areas where the two styles have been partially fused). If corroboration of this hypothesis is required, Plate 22 may perhaps provide it, for the Baluba are the only African tribe to have conceived a wooden dance mask in the form of a perfect hemisphere —the so-called *kifwebe* (which is simply their generic name for "mask". The purity of the form is emphasized in the best examples by the contoured decorative design which is incised and painted white; according to certain sculptured figures of men wearing such masks, they are worn in the horizontal position with the face upwards, but other accounts suggest that they may be tilted forwards.

Plates 23 and 24 represent two works from the Hemba subtribe of the Baluba whose sculpture may be regarded as the most classical form of Baluba art. The Hemba live to the west of the southern part of Lake Tanganyika and played a crucial part in the establishment of the empire of the Baluba. It may be that it was from them that the globular tendencies of Baluba art spread through the other peoples of the empire. A chief's ceremonial arrow-rest, deeply impregnated with palm oil like so many Hemba carvings, is seen in Plate 23, while Plate 24 shows the head of a more characteristically full-formed sculpture representing a male ancestor. This style has without doubt produced many of the finest of all African sculptures. To the southwest of the Hemba area are another important subtribe, the Shankadi. Their art is notable for the work of a great African master of the miniature form: the Master of the Cascade Coiffures. Plate 25 illustrates one of his finest works, a headrest supported on two apparently wrestling figures who wear their hair *en cascade*. The ingeniously balanced composition of the figures and their limbs appears to be peculiar to this artist. The larger works in this substyle are mainly chiefs' stools supported on caryatids such as that seen in Plate 26; the seat is in the form of another solid hemisphere, and the massive, bulbous thighs are in the pure Baluba tradition.

The Basongye or Basonge live in the area between the Baluba Hemba to the east and the eastern Bakuba and Bena Lulua to the west. They are the most important of the "Baluba-ized" tribes, and most of the art forms found among them are also found among the Baluba, with the important difference already noted—the tendency of Basongye forms to show the influence of the idea of the cube rather than of the sphere. The Basongye equivalents of the *kifwebe* masks (Plate 22) of the Baluba always have a square jaw which is the main feature of their design. As for human figures, which are common in both tribes, there are noteworthy differences in function, posture and sex as well as in style. Whereas those of the Baluba are mostly ancestor figures, those of the Basongye are fetishes in the strict sense. All Basongye figures are in the standing posture, whereas those of the Baluba are sometimes kneeling; and all but a handful of Basongye figures are male, whereas female figures probably predominate among the Baluba. The example seen in Plate 27 has the typical Basongye features of subject-matter—the horn to contain fetish medicine on the crown of the head as well as the receptacle carved out of the abdomen; the arms bent at right angles with the hands resting at each side of the abdominal cavity; the lozenge-shaped nose, overlaid with copper sheeting, and the figure-of-eight mouth. The artistic conception is " cubist " in character (though other Basongye substyles are more strikingly so, with more pronounced faceting of the volumes), and may also be described as " expressionist " because of its emotional power, in contrast to the generally tranquil appearance of Baluba sculpture.

The art styles of the Batetela, a large and widespread tribe to the north of the Basongye, have not yet been adequately studied, and they have too often been treated as an unimportant appendage of the Basongye. It would seem that the southern groups have a style of figure-carving which is quite close to that of their Basongye neighbours; some more northerly subtribes, however, appear to have had their own styles, simpler and more rudimentary, and owing little if anything to the Baluba or the Basongye. Their masks are rare, but have a distinctive character of their own, many of them having a cylindrical helmet form with projecting tubular eyes as in Plate 28.

No doubt the scarcity of representational art among the Batetela, and the other tribes of the great Mongo-speaking group, is to be associated with the fact that we are no longer dealing with peoples inhabiting the comparatively open country of the southern savannah but with peoples of the great rain forest. In western Africa the coastal forests are rich in art, but in central Africa the thick bush seems to have had the opposite effect and collections from this vast area are sparse indeed in the world's museums, although we have vast quantities of weapons, stools, headrests and other artifacts of utilitarian purpose even if often of beautiful form.

Among the northernmost Bantu-speaking tribes of the Congo—some of whom, such as the Ngombe, the Ngbaka and the Ababwa, have produced sculpture of considerable merit—is found a large Sudanic-speaking tribe, the Azande, whose territory is divided between the Democratic Republic of Congo, the Republic of Sudan and the Central African Republic. The dominant group, the aristocratic Avongara, have brought numerous small tribes of diverse origins under their sway and "Zande-ized" them over the past few centuries. Resistance to their power has, it seems, brought into being among the subject groups a society called Mani which has been the source in recent years of some small wooden figures of which Plate 29 is a good example. The Azande are otherwise rather deficient in visual art, though sometimes making use of art objects obtained from their much more prolific southern neighbours, the similarly Sudanic-speaking Mangbetu.

One other interesting type of wooden figure is found among the Azande, chiefly from the area of Yambio, a frontier town in the Bahr-el-Ghazal, and the pair of figures from Prague which are seen in Plate 30 are typical of these: the same style is found in heads and figures used to decorate certain Azande harps. Though they have some slight affinity with Mangbetu sculpture, they lack its invariable emphasis on the artificial deformation of the skull in a backward direction. It has also been suggested that they were made only for sale to Europeans, but several of them, including two exceptionally large ones in the British Museum, seem clearly to have been made for some kind of tribal use. Many examples have indeed clearly been made for the white man, but if the style

22

itself was developed for export, then it has far better claims to genuine originality, particularly in the excellent stylization of the arms, then any other tourist art in Africa.

In our last two illustrations we redress a slight over-simplification in the titles of our two volumes: African tribal sculpture is largely but not quite confined to the Niger-Congo river systems of Western and Central Africa. Until the early years of this century, in fact, there were still a number of tribes in eastern and southern Africa producing important sculpture (which can be found especially in German museums). Among them are the Washambala, Wanyamwezi and Wazaramo of Tanzania, the Anguru of Malawi and the Zulu of South Africa. The most accomplished and prolific sculptors of this vast area, however, were the Makonde group of southern Tanzania and northern Mozambique, whose traditional skills survived until the Second World War. (For this reason they have been able to make the most craftsmanlike contribution to the artistically worthless " tourist art " of East Africa.) These tribes are at first sight exceptions to the sculptural dichotomy of Africa, but this impression may be illusory, since most, if not all, of them have some kind of historical connection with the Greater Congo area and may be regarded as its outliers.

The peculiar contribution of the Makonde and related peoples to the immense variety of African sculptural styles is well illustrated in Plates 31 and 32—a kind of intensified realism verging on what Europeans would call caricature; it is easy to find curious analogues in their masks for the conventional exaggerations of the age of Hogarth and Rowlandson, or of Daumier. Helmet masks such as our Yao (Plate 31) and Makonde examples—curiously suggestive in their general design of some Gelede masks of the western Yoruba of Nigeria—are worn in the dances of the men's society. In the most recent masks the tendency to caricature has been carried to excessive lengths, the exaggeration of details destroying the harmony of the whole, but these two earlier works and many others of their period are by no means inferior to the best of West African art.

That the general absence of tribal sculpture among the eastern and southern peoples of Africa is not due to any inferiority in artistic capacity is sufficiently proved by the remarkable and spontaneous aptitude for sculpture (to quote a pre-eminent example) of the contemporary African artists working in Rhodesia under the inspiration of Frank McEwen without the benefit of any tradition of visual art. It is needless to remind ourselves that much of the finest tribal music comes from eastern Africa; and the same is true of poetry and oral literature in general, although all these and other non-visual arts are fast vanishing without trace before any serious effort has been made to record or study them. A people may indeed lose their arts under the stress of cultural change (such as Africa is undergoing), but it is improbable that they can lose the capacity for art. And no one can say where lie the limits of art within the culture of man.

ILLUSTRATIONS

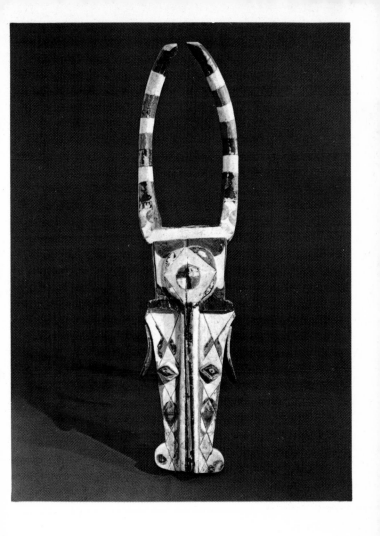

1

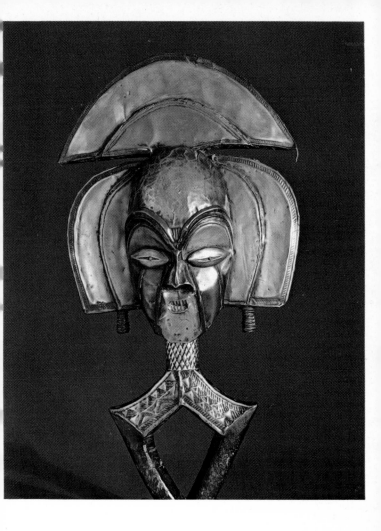

4

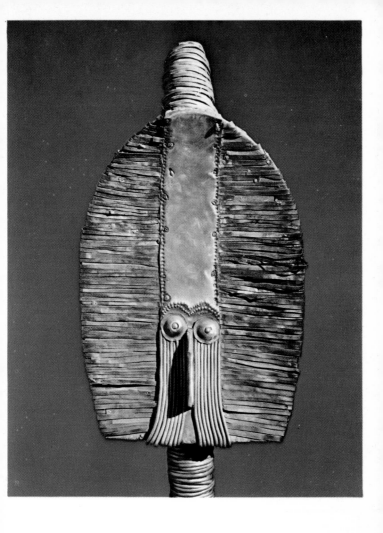

6

9

13

15

19

24

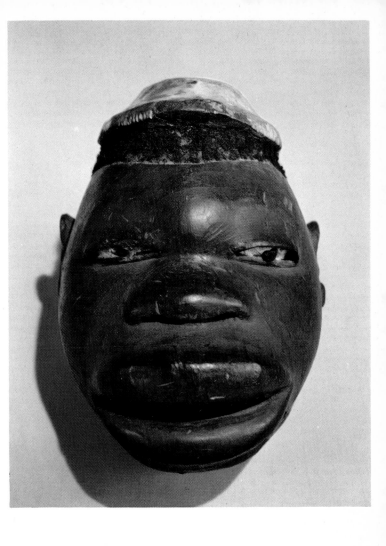

CONTENTS

Continued overleaf ▶

CONTENTS

The colour photographs for this volume were specially taken by Mario Carrieri.

Printed in Italy